Paul'

by Ruth Renelo

illustrated by Al Lorenz

Scott Foresman
is an imprint of

PEARSON

Glenview, Illinois • Boston, Massachusetts • Chandler, Arizona
Upper Saddle River, New Jersey

Every effort has been made to secure permission and provide appropriate credit for photographic material. The publisher deeply regrets any omission and pledges to correct errors called to its attention in subsequent editions.

Unless otherwise acknowledged, all photographs are the property of Scott Foresman, a division of Pearson Education.

Photo locators denoted as follows: Top (T), Center (C), Bottom (B), Left (L), Right (R), Background (Bkgd)

Illustrations by Albert Lorenz

Photographs 16 Corbis Media

ISBN 13: 978-0-328-50752-8
ISBN 10:   0-328-50752-0

8 9 10 V010 14 13

When people need wood, they cut down the trees. People who cut down trees for a living are called lumberjacks. Long ago, as lumberjacks worked, they made up tall tales. Many of these tales were about Paul Bunyan. He was the biggest and strongest make-believe lumberjack of all!

Most stories about Paul Bunyan were about his grown-up life. But some of the tales start with Paul as a baby. And what an amazing baby he was, or so the story goes!

Paul was way too big for a baby bed. He was even too big for his parents' bed. Paul was a huge baby!

"What will we do?" Paul's mother moaned. A neighbor pulled a rowboat up to the Bunyans' cabin. The boat made a fine bed for Paul. But by the end of a week, Paul had grown as big as a moose.

"What bed will be big enough?" his father asked.

Paul's parents decided to build a bed the shape and size of a sailing ship. They thought this would be big enough for their gigantic son. By then, Paul had grown as big as the family cabin. Again, the neighbors came to help.

When the ship bed was finished, they all knew it would not fit inside the cabin. So they pushed Paul's bed down to the lake and floated it on the water. They dropped an anchor so it would not float away. Then they all followed Paul as he toddled down to his new bed.

It was a snug fit, but Paul used his ship bed all summer long. When summer turned to fall, there was a new problem. They had already used every blanket they had to cover Paul. But this was not enough!

Paul was too big to fit in a cabin, where he could sleep by a warm fire. Paul's parents knew they had to find a way to keep him warm on the lake.

"We must attempt to make a huge blanket," they decided.

Again, neighbors came from miles around to help the Bunyans and their huge son. They all thought and thought about the problem. Then someone suggested they could sew together sails from ships to make a big enough quilt.

Everyone worked hard on Paul's quilt. It was quite an event. They all laughed when hundreds and hundreds of chickens came. They were carrying piles of their spare feathers to stuff inside the sail quilt.

As time passed, Paul's ship beds and quilts kept getting bigger. When he was sixteen, his ship bed was as big as the whole lake.

One morning, Paul stretched. His enormous body broke his ship bed! Boards flew and Paul fell into the lake with a mighty splash.

The splash made all the water fly out of the lake! The ducks and fish were stunned to suddenly be on dry land. Paul quickly scooped the water into his huge hands and refilled the lake. Then he carefully put all the ducks and fish back into it.

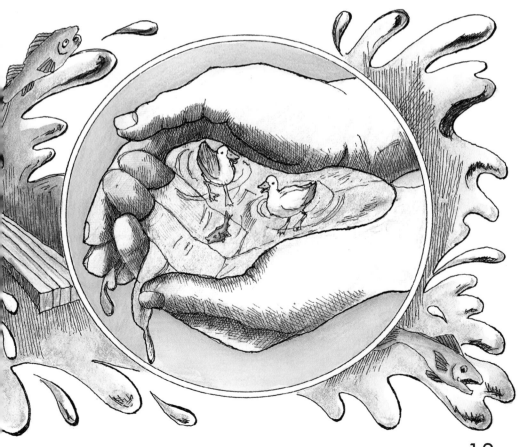

Now Paul was nearly as tall as the tallest pine tree in the woods. He knew it was up to him to find his own bed. Paul set off to gather wood to build the biggest log cabin and the biggest bed in all the land.

Paul Grows

Baby Paul

1 week old

He lived in his cabin until he grew too large once again. He knew it was time to head out to find space to live.

Paul packed a sack made from a sail and waved good-bye. He headed for deep woods and wide country. He lived happily ever after as the strongest and biggest make-believe lumberjack of all!

2 years old   16 years old

Then and Now

Real lumberjacks had to be big and strong. But they weren't giants like Paul Bunyan. They had to cut down trees using tools to help them. They often rolled the tree trunks into fast running rivers to float them down to mills. Sometimes the heavy logs were pulled out of the woods and to the mills by teams of horses or oxen.

Lumberjacks today still cut and move logs to mills. But most of the time they use machines such as hand-held chainsaws, huge clippers, and claws on giant-sized wheels to help them cut. Then they use big, heavy cranes, lifters, and trucks to move the logs out of the woods.